HEATHCLIFF
DOES IT AGAIN!

by
Geo Gately

CHARTER BOOKS, NEW YORK

HEATHCLIFF DOES IT AGAIN!

A Charter Book / published by arrangement with
McNaught Syndicate, Inc.

PRINTING HISTORY
Tempo edition / January 1982
Charter Edition / July 1984

ISBN: 0-441-32225-5

Charter Books are published by The Berkley Publishing Group,
200 Madison Avenue, New York, N.Y. 10016.
PRINTED IN THE UNITED STATES OF AMERICA

"TRAFFIC ON THE BAYVILLE BRIDGE
IS ENCOUNTERING SOME DELAY..."

"NO VISITORS ALLOWED BEHIND THE FENCE!"

"HEATHCLIFF SEEMED TO ENJOY MOUNT RUSHMORE."

5-12

"HAH!...MY DOG'S GOT OL' HEATHCLIFF THIS TIME!"

"FIRST, THE GOOD NEWS...WE ENJOYED THE AQUARIUM..."

"SEE ANYTHING YOU LIKE ?!!"

"EVERY NOW AND THEN HE STOPS BY."

"OH, OH!... HERE HE COMES... OL' STICKY FINGERS!"

1975
McNaught Synd., Inc. 5-22

"AH! JUST THE MAN I'M LOOKING FOR..."

"YOUR GAME IS IMPROVING!"

"THAT LITTLE BOOTH WAS DONATED
BY A MR. HEATHCLIFF NUTMEG."

"I'LL HANDLE THIS!"

"SPEAK OF THE DEVIL!"

"THERE'S NO AWARD FOR 'BEST AT DUMPING GARBAGE CANS.'"

"WE'RE SENDING HEATHCLIFF AWAY TO CAMP."

"AND HOW ABOUT A NICE
FLEA COLLAR FOR THE KITTY?"

"THERE *ARE* NO FLEAS
ON HEATHCLIFF!"

"HEATHCLIFF!...DON'T!"

"I'LL MAKE THE DIAGNOSIS, IF YOU DON'T MIND!"

"HEATHCLIFF'S *REALLY* LEAVING HOME THIS TIME!"

"AH!...THERE'S MY BRAVE BOY!!"

"YOU'RE ALLOWED ONE PHONE CALL AND QUIT HISSING!"

"NOW, BE A GOOD KITTY AND DON'T BOTHER THOSE FISH WHILE I'M GONE!"

"I'D KEEP HIM OUT OF SCHOOL FOR A FEW DAYS...
HE LOOKS A LITTLE PALE."

"I THINK HE'S DOING 'SHE LOVES ME, SHE LOVES ME NOT!'"

"HEATHCLIFF LOVED IT!"

"SQUEAK OR TREAT?"

"ONE GOOD THING, SPIKE...YOU CAN PUT THIS UNDER YOUR PILLOW FOR THE TOOTH FAIRY."

"WOW!...YOUR GRANDMA MAKES GREAT COSTUMES!"

"HALLOWEEN WAS YESTERDAY, HEATHCLIFF!"

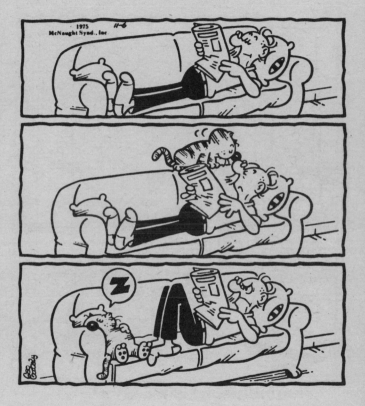

"WILL HE FIT IN THE NET?"

"HE'S A BIT OF A HYPOCHONDRIAC, ISN'T HE?"

"ARE YOU AWARE THAT MANY CATS
ARE FINICKY EATERS?"

"IF YOU DON'T MIND, *I'LL* DECIDE WHO TO SEND IN!!"

"YOU MUST EXCUSE ME, FOLKS...IT'S TIME TO
STUFF THE TURKEY."

"HEAVY DATE TONIGHT?"

"WELL, THERE GOES THE NEIGHBORHOOD!"

"WELL, YES...HE DOES HAVE A TENDENCY TO BOLT HIS FOOD."

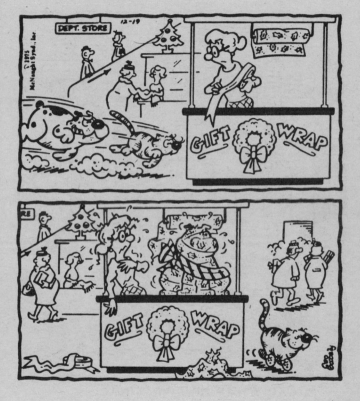

"WHAT'S HE DONE NOW ?!"

"CALM DOWN AND TELL ME WHAT HAPPENED!"

"HE WANTS YOU TO GIVE IT TO A NEEDY CAT."

"HEATHCLIFF DOESN'T LIKE THE IDEA OF REINDEER LANDING ON OUR ROOF!"

"ABOUT THIS GUARANTEED
INDESTRUCTIBLE CAT TOY..."

"DID YOU HAVE TO BRING *HIM* ALONG?"

"LOOK, GRANDMA!-SANTA ATE UP ALL THE COOKIES AND MILK WE LEFT HIM!"

"YOU'RE BEING PUNISHED!... I SAID
'NO TELEVISION FOR A WEEK!'"

"BEEN OUT ALL NIGHT SOWING A FEW WILD OATS?"

"HE DIDN'T WIN, BUT THEY VOTED HIM
'MR. CONGENIALITY'."

"I THINK HE'S DOING 'HELLO DOLLY'!"

"...AND STAY AWAY FROM THAT FISH MARKET!"

"NO!...I'M *NOT* GOING TO SHOVEL THE FENCE!"

"BABY IS TEETHING."

"WATCH YOUR THUMB, MR. KLINKER!"

"HERE COMES HEATHCLIFF WITH HIS SLED DOG!"

© 1976
McNaught
Syndicate, Inc.

1-24

"WHY, NO...I DIDN'T SEND ANYONE IN TO
INSPECT THE KITCHEN!"

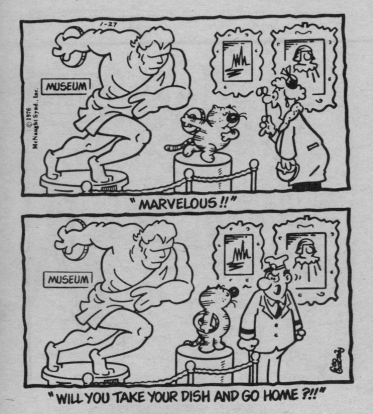

"STAIN YOUR BIB?"

"WE GOT OUR REPORT CARDS TODAY...
HEATHCLIFF IS LOOKING AT IT."

"HEATHCLIFF'S NOT GOING OUT TONIGHT."

"HEATHCLIFF IS HOLDING HEARINGS CONCERNING SPIKE'S BEHAVIOR."

"WHO ARE YOU CALLING A QUACK ?!"

"WHO SPENT $7.98 ON HEATHCLIFF'S COAT OF ARMS?!"

"NO!-YOU CAN'T SEE HER!"

"I JUST MARK 'EM THE WAY THEY PRICE 'EM!"

"HE'LL BE OUT SOON... HE'S DOING HIS DISH."

"WILL YOU LOOK AT THAT!...NOW HE'S EVEN GOT HIS OWN UNIFORM!"

"YOU'RE A CONNIVING CUSS WHO IS
EIGHT POUNDS OVERWEIGHT!"

"NOW, WHO LEFT THAT DOOR OPEN?!"

"HAS ANYONE SEEN MY WIG ?!"

"OH, OH!...WHAT'S HE DONE NOW ?!!"

"I THINK YOU CAN GET ALONG WITHOUT AN ANTIQUE SCRATCHING POST!"

"THE FIGHT'S OFF!...HEATHCLIFF NEVER
TAKES SECOND BILLING!"

"GET LOST!"

"CAN YOU BRONZE A CAT BOOTY?"

"DON'T WORRY, DEAR...WE'LL GET YOU A GOOD LAWYER."

"HE'S A MIXED BREED."

"DON'T GRAB FOR THINGS AT THE TABLE, SPIKE!"

"HEATHCLIFF IS IN HIS DRESSING ROOM."

"WOULD YOU LIKE TO TALK TO 'DIAL A PRAYER'?"

"NO, NO, SPIKE!...WATCH HOW HEATHCLIFF
HOLDS HIS CUP!"

"CAT FOOD COUPONS GO IN THE *"IN"* BASKET."

"WELL, AIN'T THAT CUTE!...LOOK WHO'S HUNTING EASTER...

...EGGS!"

"LOOK, HEATHCLIFF!...LOOK AT THE CUTE CHICKS!"

"HE'S EMBARRASSED...HE WON'T COME TO BREAKFAST IN HIS NEW SLIPPERS."

"NEVER MIND HEATHCLIFF...I THINK YOU LOOK FINE!"

"THAT'S A PERFECTLY GOOD HALF DOLLAR!"

"DO YOU HAVE A RESERVATION?!"

"HE DOESN'T NEED A LAWYER!"

"MAY I HELP YOU?"

"HEATHCLIFF'S HAVING HIS BED RE-UPHOLSTERED."

" I'M A BIT FED UP WITH HIS
'HOLIER THAN THOU' ATTITUDE! "

"OH, WOW!....MADEMOISELLE FIFI'S BUBBLE BATH!"

"WE'RE QUITE SATISFIED WITH OUR PRESENT MASCOT, THANK YOU!"

"NO THANKS...YOUR OWNER CAN PAY THE BILL!"

"HE LIKED THIS ONE!...HE GAVE IT A GOLD STAR!"

"SPIKE!...YOU *KNOW* HEATHCLIFF DOESN'T
APPROVE OF DUNKING!"

"LOOKOUT, HEATHCLIFF!...THE LIFEGUARD
IS COMING BACK!"

"IS THAT ALL HE CAN SAY?... 'THE SKY IS FALLING!'?"

"OH, BROTHER!...WAIT'LL YOU SEE THE PROGRAM
FOR TONIGHT'S CONCERT!"

"WHAT CAN I DO?!....ITS HIS OWN SAFETY DEPOSIT BOX!"